CHARLESTON ICONS

CHARLESTON ICONS

50 SYMBOLS OF THE HOLY CITY

Ida A. Becker

Guilford, Connecticut

Spoleto Festival photos p. 10–11 courtesy of Spoleto Festival USA
Dock Street Theatre photo p. 18 (bottom) courtesy of Charleston Area
Convention and Vistors Bureau, CVB, www.charlestoncvb.com
All other interior photos © Ida A. Becker

Project editor: Jessica Haberman
Text design and layout: Casey Shain

Library of Congress Cataloging-in-Publication Data
Becker, Ida A.
 Charleston icons : 50 symbols of the Holy City / Ida A. Becker.
  p. cm.
 ISBN 978-0-7627-4799-3
 1. Charleston (S.C.)—Civilization. 2. Charleston (S.C.)—Social life and customs. 3. Charleston (S.C.)—Description and travel. 4. Historic buildings—South Carolina— Charleston. 5. Historic sites—South Carolina—Charleston. 6. Charleston (S.C.)— Buildings, structures, etc. I. Title.
 F279.C45B43 2009
 917.57'9150444—dc22

                                                                                    2009013728

Printed in China
10 9 8 7 6 5 4 3 2 1

*To the charm and grace of Charleston that has
lured so many, myself included, home again.*

CONTENTS

INTRODUCTION

I had the spectacular good fortune of being born to a city that is latitudinarian in its ideals, hallmarked by its seaside idyll, and populated by generations of indefatigably proud people. Charleston is a cocoon of gentility surrounded by a sensuous landscape of verdant tea olives, majestic magnolias, and undulating coastal dunes that we lovingly call the Lowcountry. Prized for its well-preserved, palimpsest architecture, the city is a veritable living museum, and Charlestonians who trace their roots back several generations are often vernacular stylists who punctuate the air with a plumy southern drawl

and charmingly peculiar pronunciations of words such as *Legare* (Luh-gree), *Gaillard* (Gil-yard), *Cooper* (Cup-puh), and *Prioleau* (Pray-low). Although savored for its antediluvian charm, the city is bustling with the vigor of artists, chefs, and visionaries focused on advancing the area's aerospace, automotive, biosciences, and creative industries, all of whom have affirmed Charleston's deserved reputation as an epicenter of culture, a sumptuous dining destination, and a hub of ingenuity.

In May 2007, I sailed out of our picturesque harbor aboard a 70-foot Swan competing in the biennial Charleston to Bermuda Race. The view of the receding skyline and encircling barrier islands from offshore was a poignant panorama and a reminder of the region's entwining history with the sea. It was upon these waters that Charleston's first wave of colonists arrived in 1670, bringing with them a tolerant temperament, reverence for the past, and an optimistic eye toward the future, traits that endowed the city with the distinctive joie de vivre we celebrate today.

CHARLESTON ICONS

CHARLESTON HARBOR

The crack of a sail catching the wind; *the swish of the waves washing about the stern; the creak of timber pitching yardarm to yardarm:* These were the sounds of the colonists' star-bound journey to the new world. It was a tempestuous passage that began with a blue sea dream, coursed across an unforgiving ocean that claimed two of the three ships in the fleet, and ended in piquant waters. Sight of the peaceful harbor likely provided incredible mental salve to the *mal de mer* of the British settlers who, after seven months of sailing, arrived in what would become Charles Towne. The year was 1670. As the battered schooner limped to mooring, no one aboard could have guessed that within 100 years' time, their new port would eclipse New York City's annual export tonnage and Charles Towne would be the new world's most prosperous city.

Spirit of South Carolina www.scmaritime .org

The oceangoing freighters that pull into the Charleston Harbor today are among the largest traversing international waters, and shipping continues to be one of the region's dominant sources of economic stimulation. Meanwhile, the modern commercial port dwarfs the wooden mast of the *Spirit of South Carolina,* a majestic tall ship crafted by local shipwrights that evokes imagery of the colonial maritime era when local tramps ferried goods from upriver plantations to vessels bound for foreign shores.

If waves could scribe, the harbor's waters would yield annals of history, a deluge of firsthand accounts that annotate the city's evolution. From its role as a watery battlefield on which pivotal naval campaigns played out during both the American Revolution and the Civil War to today's more placid role in commerce and recreation, the harbor is teeming with stories.

PALMETTO TREE

There's something poetic about the Palmetto, its silvery silhouette pinned to swaths of royal blue fabric that soar above the city; something unexpected: notoriety born from a floral fable that involved war and superpower strength; something intriguing: a clutch of aliases, including Sabal Palmetto, Cabbage Palmetto, and Palmetto Palm; and something hardy: It's the drought-tolerant camel of trees that's equally undaunted by saltwater.

Its lore began on June 28, 1776, when the Patriots waged a decisive victory over the British during the opening stages of the American Revolution. A meager phalanx of several hundred freedom fighters were hunkered down in the palmetto-log and sandbag fort on Sullivan's Island, the flank of land on the eastern entrance of the harbor, when nine British warships carrying more than one thousand soldiers arrived. Over the course of the daylong battle, Commander William Moultrie and his men marveled at the surprising elasticity of the logs, which absorbed the

Fort Moultrie
1214 Middle
Street
www.nps.gov/
fomo

M. Dumas & Sons
294 King Street
(843) 723-8600

shock of the incoming cannonballs. The Patriots, safely sequestered behind the rudimentary yet resilient fortification, were able to return fire with exacting precision. The heavily damaged armada retreated. In an auspicious show of gallantry, Sergeant William Jasper leapt into the line of fire in order to salvage the Patriots' fallen flag, then just a blue field featuring a crescent moon. When South Carolina seceded from the nation on the eve of the Civil War, the symbolic palmetto tree was stitched onto the flag to harken the pivotal success at Fort Moultrie. This design has served as the official state flag ever since, and the palmetto was adopted as the official state tree in 1939.

Its rustling fronds are ubiquitous across the Lowcountry thanks to the city's beautification efforts and the tree's inherent ability to thrive in a brackish environment; however, it is even more abundant in the proliferation of M. Dumas & Sons' native pride apparel—hats, belts, shirts, and the like—that bear a monogram of the knave palmetto.

PORGY AND BESS

Set amid the shabby beauty of a manse-turned-tenement called Catfish Row, a colorful ghetto teeming with hucksters and lonely hearts, the hard-scrabble life of Charleston's slums springs to life with heart-wrenching detail in the Dreiserian tale of crippled Porgy and battered Bess.

Based on native son DuBose Heyward's novel *Porgy*, considered by biographer James M. Hutchisson to be "the first major southern novel to portray blacks without condescension," and set to music by Tin Pan Alley maestro George Gershwin, *Porgy and Bess* was a groundbreaking folk opera that immortalized the struggle of working-class blacks in the south during the Jazz Age.

Heyward and Gershwin whiled away the summer of 1934 on Folly Beach, giving the Brooklyn-born composer an opportunity to absorb the lolling, Spanish moss–drenched Lowcountry lifestyle. Inspired by Gullah

music and the joyous bedlam of church revivals, he melded the dulcet sounds of Charleston into his sweeping score.

The show made its debut in 1935 with a cast comprised entirely of African-American actors. It alighted to Broadway's Alvin Theatre on October 10, where it ran for 124 performances before launching an east coast tour. While in Washington, D.C., the cast successfully protested segregation, which resulted in the first integrated audience at the National Theatre.

While not a tremendous financial success, Gershwin considered *Porgy and Bess* to be his seminal work, and the haunting nocturne *Summertime* has been embraced by singers of nearly every genre, from Billie Holiday to Janis Joplin. *Porgy and Bess* was proclaimed the official opera of the state of South Carolina in 2001, and it was inducted into the Library of Congress in 2003 for its cultural, historical, and aesthetic significance.

CHARLESTON RENAISSANCE

"Come quickly, have found heaven,*"* was the succinct, beseeching message artist Alfred Hutty wired to his wife upon discovering the auspicious charms of Charleston in 1919. Hired to establish an art school for the Carolina Art Association, the acclaimed painter found the city ripe for artistic nurturing during a Beaux Arts era that spanned from 1920 to 1945.

During the Charleston Renaissance, a constellation of artistic visionaries articulated the city's aura with pens, paintbrushes, and etching knives. Some exalted her grandeur, while others dismantled the archaic image of a haughty, ennobled city.

Equally paradoxical were the artists who defined this movement: They were not all South-born. Some, like Josephine Pinckney and DuBose Heyward, were anointed with storied surnames that stood for an illustrious local lineage; others—including Hutty—were parvenu to the Holy City. Collectively, they were a prolific coterie of poets, painters, playwrights, preservationists, and writers, many of whom gathered for lively literary salons hosted by then

Gibbes Museum 135 Meeting Street www.gibbes museum.org

director of the Charleston Museum, Laura Bragg.

Their éclat cast far-reaching ripples throughout the community that resulted in the founding of the Poetry Society, the Charleston Etchers' Club, the Southern States Art League, the Society for the Preservation of Old Dwellings, and several art schools. Their names— Elizabeth O'Neill Verner, Alice Ravenel Huger, Emmett Robinson, Dorothy Heyward, Hervey Allen, Archibald Rutledge, Beatrice St. Julien Ravenel, Herbert Ravenel Sass, and Susan Pringle Frost—are an intrinsic part of Charleston's cultural commentary.

A variety of exemplary works from the era, including 247 pieces credited to Hutty, are housed in the permanent collection at the Gibbes Museum of Art, a finely detailed Beaux Arts building in the heart of downtown. Meanwhile, the most esteemed award bestowed upon the arts in South Carolina bears the name of Verner, whose illustrations for Heyward's *Porgy* provided an accurate and compelling peek at the real-life inspiration behind the gritty southern drama.

SPOLETO FESTIVAL USA
AND PICCOLO SPOLETO

Ask a Charlestonian to describe Spoleto Festival USA and you might be regaled with the memory of honey-throated songbird Ella Fitzgerald warbling at a gibbon moon during a midnight performance on the lawn of the College of Charleston. Or perhaps you'll hear the story of a heart-stopping high-wire act that sent one of Circus Flora's Flying Wallendas dancing across the void between City Hall and the adjacent post office—without a safety net!

A frisson of color and sound seizes the city for seventeen days every spring when internationally renowned artists descend upon the city for both Spoleto and its "little sister," Piccolo Spoleto, an effort by the city's Office of Cultural Affairs to produce family-friendly, affordable events compared to Spoleto's more esoteric fare.

During the festivals, Charlestonians jettison their savored slow pace of life preferring to kinetically crisscross the city at all hours of the day and night, commencing with chamber music

Spoleto Festival USA
www.spoletousa
.org
(843) 579-3100

Piccolo Spoleto
www.piccolo
spoleto.com
(843) 724-7305

after morning coffee and carrying on through invitation-only cast parties that stretch into the wee hours of the following dawn.

A cyclorama of opera, dance, theater, poetry, visual arts, and concerts, Spoleto annually presents 120 performances, while Piccolo boasts 700 events in its festival slate. Every city venue is monopolized during the festival and even inspired spaces—like the shaded lawn beneath a majestic Angel Oak tree estimated to be more than 1,500 years old—are treated to a performance of some sort.

Spoleto has debuted more than 100 world premieres since its founding in 1977, including *Creve Coeur* by Tennessee Williams, *The American Clock* by Arthur Miller, and *Hydrogen Jukebox* by Philip Glass and Allen Ginsberg. Piccolo, too, has launched its fair share of premieres and even inspired its own offshoot—Piccolo Fringe, a comedy improv series that runs concurrent with the festival.

JOGGLING BOARD

The alchemy of the joggling board, a frothy rocking chair–bench hybrid, is rooted in amorous lore: Courting couples would spend hours demurely bouncing toward one another for a furtive kiss before joggling back to their respective ends of board. Its origin, however, is distinctively uncoquettish. Created in the early 1830s as a purported therapy for rheumatism, its sway providing a gentle form of exercise, the bizarre bouncing contraption quickly captured the attention of Charlestonians. Its novel appeal made it a fashionable piazza adornment, while its straightforward construction contributed to its rampant popularity.

Traditionally a sixteen-foot piece of pliable pine pegged between two rockers and given a sturdy coat of Charleston Green paint, joggling boards can safely hold up to three adults according to a feature that appeared in *Popular Science* in 1941, which heralded the pastime as a "popular source of amusement for friends and neighbors." The article included a blueprint for do-it-yourself woodwork-

*Old Charleston Joggling Board Company
652 King Street
www.joggling board.com
(843) 723-4331*

ers that kept the 100-year-old novelty going when commercial production of joggling boards ceased due to resource scarcity during World War II.

In 1959 Charlestonian Thomas E. Thornhill sought a joggling board for his new home on Tradd Street, but when he failed to find one in stores, he fashioned his own. During South Carolina's tercentennial in 1970, Thornhill resurrected this bit of southern-born Americana when he and Leonard C. Fulghum, a painting contractor, founded the Old Charleston Joggling Board Company.

Avant-garde dance impresario Martha Graham gave the board a jolt of notoriety when she incorporated one as a central part of the choreography in *Maple Leaf Rag,* her quirky 1990 season-opening production. Graham had discovered the whimsical boards when her troupe of dancers appeared at the 1989 Spoleto Festival USA, and three years after its NYC debut, a reprisal of *Maple Leaf Rag,* Graham's last completed dance before her death in 1991, was staged for Spoleto.

CHARLESTON SINGLE HOUSE

Amid the pastiche of styles that make the city a stunning repository of architectural wonder, the single house is an archetypal legacy unto itself. Designed to suit the whims of Charleston's steamy summers, the distinctive vernacular of the typically two-story structure consists of wide, shutter-lined piazzas intended to capture the passing sea breezes. As aesthetically pleasing as it is functional, the single house measures only one room deep on both floors, thus the piazzas double as living spaces, most commonly as sleeping porches during the height of summer heat.

Yellow pine and cypress harvested from nearby forests and floated to Charleston on an ebb tide—a passage that rendered the planks cured by the salt water and incredibly hard—replaced brick and tabby as the construction

Charleston Strolls
www.charleston
strolls.com
(843) 766-2080

material of choice for peninsula dwellings. The compact design parlayed well to the needs of a growing population that required housing on the peninsula.

By the eighteenth century, the single house was the predominant floor plan among new construction.

Much of the original wood siding has survived the past 200 years of storms and pestilence and can be seen during a walking tour of the Lower Peninsula. The most authentic examples are found in the heart of the peninsula, most notably at 18 Meeting Street, 14 Legare Street, and 71 Church Street—the oldest single house in the city. Interestingly, the unique floor plan is ideal for urban density and in a *what's-old-is-new-again* renewal, the single-home design is populating neotraditional communities across the Lowcountry.

SEERSUCKER SUITS

A sartorial relic, Charleston survives as the last bastion of seersucker, where dandies stroll down Broad Street festooned in the eponymous striped suits, foppish bowties, white suede buckskin lace-ups with red rubber soles, and straw boaters—the picture of Atticus Finch in _To Kill a Mockingbird_.

A colorful term meaning "milk and sugar," seersucker originated in Persia, far from the Lowcountry's textile mills, but the crinkly cotton, with its signature cornflower blue stripe, gained rampant popularity during the British colonial period due to its breathability in a humid climate.

Seersucker requires a bit of bravado to wear. It's one of the few fabrics worn in a wrinkly state, and no amount of ironing will "undo" the signature pucker. The breezy

M. Dumas & Sons
294 King Street
(843) 723-8603

style is _de rigueur_ attire for steamy outdoor southern weddings as well as the third Thursday in June when senators in the U.S. Congress don the lightweight fabric to "bring a little southern charm to the Capitol," a tradition that recalls the legislative wardrobe prior to the invention of air conditioning. The distinctive fabric may only make a once-yearly appearance at the Capitol, but bon viveurs don seersucker May through September.

Although luxe French couture house Hermes has produced a men's seersucker suit (with a searing price tag of $3,000), locals outfit themselves at M. Dumas & Sons, a locally owned gentleman's clothier that opened for business in 1917 and has been helmed by three generations of the Dumas family.

DOCK STREET THEATRE

Absurdist farce. Biting political satire. Contemporary commentaries. Inspired original works. Musical showboats. The panoply of theatricalities that has treaded the boards at the corner of Church and Queen Streets, site of America's first permanent playhouse, is fetchingly considerable.

Although Charleston's luminous legacy of patronizing the performing arts began soon after the city's founding, with taverns doubling as performance spaces, construction of the Dock Street in 1736 ushered in a new era of entertainment. The inaugural production, a wildly bawdy play called *The Recruiting Officer,* thrilled theater patrons who responded with an overwhelming request for ticket subscriptions, but the fanfare was short-lived: The theater was reduced to cinder by a fire that engulfed the entire French Quarter only four years after its debut.

A potent rum concoction called Planter's Punch replaced onstage pageantry during the site's second act, when a spectacular three-story brick and stucco hotel—the building seen

Charleston Stage
135 Church
Street
www.charleston
stage.com
(843) 577-7183

today with its immediately identifiable wrought-iron balcony, brownstone columns, and black and white checked portico—rose from the ashes. The Planter's Inn became the darling of plantation folk who visited town for the sporting season, but in the wake of the Civil War, the haute lodging fell into disrepair. An intermission spanning several decades ensued.

The third act commenced in the 1930s when the building was resurrected as a theater under a Works Progress Administration directive. The restored theater opened in 1937 with a reprisal of *The Recruiting Officer,* which helped ignite a renaissance of the arts in Charleston.

In 2007 the city of Charleston launched a $20 million restoration project intended to augment current facilities, improve handicap accessibility, and stabilize the structure against seismic activity. Construction is expected to finish in 2010, when Charleston Stage, the resident company, will once again light up the stage with more than 100 performances a year.

RENOVATION OF

DOCK STREET THEATRE

HONORABLE JOSEPH P. RILEY, JR., MAYOR

· CITY COUNCIL MEMBERS ·

ANNE FRANCES BLEECKER

YVONNE D. EVANS

HENRY B. FISHBURNE, JR.

JIMMY S. GALLANT, III

WENDELL G. GILLIARD

JAMES LEWIS, JR.

CITY COUNCIL MEMBERS ·

ROBERT M. MITCHELL

DEBORAH MORINELLI

LARRY D. SHIRLEY

PAUL C. TINKLER

LOUIS L. WARING

KATHLEEN G. WILSON

City of Charleston

BUILT IN 1809 · CURRENT THEATRE ESTABLISHED 1935

TEA

A gossamer cloud of silken-winged butterflies appears each year on Wadmalaw Island heralding the end of the harvest at the Charleston Tea Plantation, the only farm of its kind in North America. As the clipped tea leaves are moved into the warehouse for drying, the butterflies tipple the nectar from the fragrant young blossoms. By the time the resplendent denizens have flown off in search of other late estival blooms, sachets of American Tea are ready for brewing.

Drinking tea is perhaps the oldest tradition in Charleston. An import from mother England, colonists maintained their staunch love for tea and afternoon teatime, a soothing ritual touchstone amid the turbulent new world. It did not, however, take long for the unassuming beverage to become a divisive tool of control. To quash the colonist's fledgling acts of independence, British Parliament allowed the East India Company to hold a monopoly on the tea trade in America while levying a stiff tariff on imported tea.

Charleston Tea Plantation
6617 Maybank Highway
Wadmalaw Island
www.charleston teaplantation.com
(843) 559-0383

In December 1773, a ship laden with 257 caches of tea sailed into the Charles Towne harbor. The Liberty Boys, a self-titled band of independence rabblers, called forth an emergency town meeting to discuss the tea tariff and its crown-control implications. Although public sympathy sided with the boycott, three prominent merchants—John Savage, Miles Brewton, and David Deas—took the opportunity to form the Charles Towne Chamber of Commerce with the intent of opposing the tea standoff. The result? The act of aggression was a harbinger of the American Revolution, the Chamber of Commerce survives today as the oldest such organization in the United States, and people are still drinking tea.

Ambrosial, cognac-colored, and best when served over ice in a mason jar, sweet tea is the nectar running through Charlestonians' veins. Adoration of the drink extends as far as an official proclamation by the state legislature naming it as "the official hospitality beverage" of South Carolina.

OLD SLAVE MART MUSEUM

The handsome, weathered exterior of the heather gray stucco-over-brick building belies the stormy history housed inside this degraded auction gallery turned museum.

The engine at the nucleus of Charleston's economic livelihood, slavery radically shaped the city's rise to prosperity, but complaints from white residents living in proximity to the unseemly cargo deliveries brought about an ordinance mandating that slaves could not be sold in view of the public. Overnight, human chattel auction houses, like the one at 6 Chalmers Street that belonged to former sheriff Thomas Ryan, sprang up in the neighborhood surrounding the Old Exchange. Despite the slave trade's metastasizing hold on Charleston, vestiges of Ryan's Mart are the only existing remnants of the nefarious transaction sites.

Originally comprised of a brick walled yard, a three-story barracoon that housed slaves prior to the sale, a kitchen, and a morgue, only a few of the original structure's walls have survived the erosion of time. The last slave sale took place in November 1863, and ownership

Old Slave Mart Museum
6 Chalmers Street
(843) 958-6467

of the property turned over many times in the years following the Civil War. Recognizing its immense, albeit tragic, role in history, the city of Charleston purchased the building in 1988 and contemplated its use for nearly two decades. On October 31, 2007, the Old Slave Mart Museum, an exhibition of objects and narratives related to the heritage of the early Africans, opened its doors to the public.

Inside, two floors of exhibits paint a portrait of a society struggling to carve out its autonomy but doing so on the backs of indentured men. Oral histories and personal letters chronicle the perilous middle passage of the African diaspora who liken Charleston, the port of entry for forty percent of all slaves dispersed throughout the British colonies, to Ellis Island. Hauntingly reprehensible artifacts—shackles and a neck collar—illustrate the monstrous nature of men enslaving fellow men. But with an eye toward a more harmonious future, an inspirational account of strength among the slaves reminds visitors of the human will to survive and thrive.

SHE CRAB SOUP

The bisque's austere blanched hue camouflages its frisson of flavor. Dense morsels of Atlantic blue crab are cocooned in a cream-based bisque that plays up the meat's tantalizing sweetness. The dish is finished with a splash of dry sherry and a dash of zest: roe that is as shocking for its bright orange color as its salty crunch.

Believed to have originated with Scottish immigrants in the 1700s who adapted their old-world partan bree seafood stew recipe to accommodate a new-world flavor, the simple preparation of crab soup spiced with Madeira made for a hearty meal. It was William Deas, the butler of Mrs. Goodwyn Rhett, an entertaining doyenne, who reportedly added roe, a panache befitting a presidential palette according to tour guide lore, which ascribes the addition of the colorful eggs as an attempt to impress a visiting President Taft.

Harvesting roe from a "berried" crab, a mature female with a visible spongelike pouch, is now illegal, so the dish requires the substitution of unfertilized eggs from immature crabs or boiled eggs in a pinch. Over the years, chefs

82 Queen
82 Queen Street
www.82queen
.com

have styled the soup to serve their personal palate with versions ranging from kicky cayenne concoctions to sweet iterations spiked with copious amounts of sherry.

In an annual competition held by the *Charleston City Paper,* a weekly entertainment newspaper, readers have consistently voted 82 Queen's she crab soup as the best in the city.

82 Queen's recipe, as published on the restaurant's Web site:

Roux: ¼ pound butter, ¼ pound flour

Ingredients:
1 cup heavy cream
3 cups milk
2 cups fish stock or water and fish base
¼ pound crab roe
1 pound white crabmeat (special)
1 cup chopped celery, light sautéed with:
   ¼ cup chopped carrots
   ¼ cup chopped onion
   ¼ cup sherry wine
   1 tablespoon Tabasco sauce
   1 tablespoon Worcestershire sauce

Preparation: Melt butter, stir in flour. Add milk and cream. Bring to a boil. Add remaining ingredients. Simmer for 20 minutes. Garnish with sherried whipped cream.

Charleston
SHE-CRAB SOUP

2 CUPS WHITE CRAB MEAT AND CRAB ROE —
FEW DROPS ONION JUICE — 1 Qt. MILK — 1/4 LB.
BUTTER — 1/4 PT. CREAM (WHIPPED) — MACE—SALT
PEPPER — 1 TBS. FLOUR — 1/2 TSP. WORCESTERSHIRE
SAUCE — 4 TBS. DRY SHERRY — MELT BUTTER AND
BLEND FLOUR — ADD MILK — CRABMEAT — ROE — AND
ALL SEASONING EXCEPT SHERRY — COOK SLOWLY
OVER HOT WATER FOR 20 MIN. — ADD 1/2 TBS.
WARMED SHERRY TO INDIVIDUAL SOUP BOWLS —
ADD SOUP AND TOP EACH SERVING WITH
WHIPPED CREAM — SERVE HOT!   GAILLARD ORIGINALS

GULLAH

A mystical tongue that bobs and weaves with dramatic intonation, staccato cadence, and linguistic peculiarities seemingly impossible to parse upon first sound, Gullah is a lyrical patois born of a colorful provenance consisting of several languages cobbled together: Sierra Leone's Krio, Nigerian Pidgen, a Bahamian dialect, and Jamaican Creole. But it's not just a Lowcountry language; Gullah refers to the direct ancestors of slaves imported from the Windward Coast of Africa and their wonderfully preserved culture, which includes crafts, superstitions, religion, medicine, food, and unique way of life.

A hardy, self-reliant people who fashioned the tools needed to prosper in the coastal plains from the bounty of natural resources readily available in the Lowcountry; from hand-woven fishing nets and sweetgrass baskets to quilts with familial stories sewn between the seams, Gullah handicrafts are the living historical record of a populace that has existed for generations in the relative isolation of Charleston's sea islands.

The Gullah people have thrived not only in life but also in death. Believing

Gullah Tours
www.gullahtours
.com

that a person's soul is returned to its maker but that the meddlesome spirit remains on earth, the culture is rich in afterlife folklore. Don't misunderstand if you ask a local to explain the blue paint on a veranda ceiling. Charlestonians aren't a sardonic bunch telling you that it *"ain't blue!"* They're saying, *"haint blue."* The spirits of the dead—haints—abound, and this distinctive hue is thought to ward off unwelcome supernatural visitors.

Salvation from the nefarious spirits was often sought at praise houses, a mostly bygone institution of joyous bedlam during which elders led the community in a ring shout, a volley of revelatory clapping, ecclesiastical shouting, and dancing. But when prayers alone were not enough to cure someone's woes, Gullah turn to root doctors for help with spells or to grannies, community healers who developed methods of healing physical ailments drawn from the indigenous Lowcountry flora. The Gullah's measure of living off the land is the bricolage of their bucolic lifestyle, and one that endures to this day.

NET. WT. 6 oZ/169.80.

GULLAH GOURMET Inc.™
CHARLESTON, SC 29407

CITY MARKET

Bloated buzzards and rancid offal rendered the meat market at the corner of Broad and Meeting Streets an urban blight. The air was ripe with discarded fish entrails at the Queen Street seafood market. Daily vegetable purchases required yet a third stop at the market on Tradd Street. Thanks to an effort spearheaded by prominent statesman Charles Cotesworth Pinckney in 1788, which ceded land to the city with the stipulation that it always be used as a municipal market, Charlestonians were able to stock their larders with a stop to one place: Centre Market.

Drawn in by the lyrical lure of Gullah vendors hawking vegetables, meat, and seafood— *Wegitubble! Bakein! Swimp!*—Charlestonians flocked to the open-air market spanning several blocks along the market's eponymous street throughout the nineteenth century. The stands and stalls, which rented for roughly $.02 to $1.33 per day, thrived for nearly 100 years after opening in

*The City Market
Market Street*

1807, perhaps due to the stiff $20 fine levied on anyone caught selling comestibles from a place other than Centre Market. But as the population spread past the market, the former delineation of the city's northern boundary, small neighborhood grocers jockeyed for business. The main market lost its luster and gave rise to tattoo parlors and blind tigers. A tornado in 1938 denigrated the area further, and it remained a floundering eyesore until the '70s, when a popular flea market sparked a resurgence.

Vendors no longer sell fresh food, but the presence of Gullah lingers in the form of sweetgrass basket weavers who tout their remarkable handicraft amid a smorgasbord of curios. However, the City Market, as it is now called, is on the eve of another renaissance thanks to the effort of a few local businessmen who, in recognizing the value of Market Street as one of the city's vital commercial corridors, have pledged to restore some of its former glory.

CAROLINA GOLD RICE

Billowing fields of golden stalks, the earthy escutcheon of Charleston's baronial hinterlands, gave rise to the richest city in the nation by the end of the American Revolution while also begetting a distinct culture and cuisine intimately woven to the cultivation of rice.

The colony's first economic supercrop made its way to local shores by fortuitous happenstance. A small quantity of Madagascar rice seed was exchanged for repairs to a storm-battered sailing vessel in 1680, and the crop thrived in the Lowcountry's quaggy soil. The mature rice revealed a surprising starch quality that, depending on cooking conditions, could yield one of three different textures—sticky, creamy, or separate grain. The versatility of this novel propagation appealed to the global market, and within fifty year's time, Charleston was exporting more than twenty million pounds of rice per year, affirming it as the world's leading rice exporter.

Anson Mills
www.ansonmills
.com
(803) 467-4122

Following the American Revolution, a savvy marketer renamed the ubiquitous local rice Carolina Gold, an umbrella moniker for the Lowcountry's unique long grains, and the term Carolina Rice has been a globally recognized classification ever since.

With a resplendent nutty flavor that deigns all modern hybrid rice a bland lot, Carolina Gold is the superstar ingredient in many heirloom recipes, but some locals take great delight in the castoffs of the annual harvest. In the argot of the rice harvesting "middlins" or "rice grits" are the grains that fracture during the exhaustive hulling, willowing, and polishing process. These broken, lesser-quality grains were historically removed from the bushel and set aside for local pantries but are said to be a better flavor absorber and a more popular choice than their whole grain brethren. Recipes abound on the Anson Mills Web site, one of the few farms that still produces the labor-intensive artisanal rice.

CAROLINA

From the Pee Dee River at   Plumfield Plantation

AROMATIC RICE

PLANTATION

1 LB.
NET WT.

PLANTATIONS

Like the dazzling blue-green plumage of a peacock, plantation lands fanned out across Charleston's alluvial marshlands throughout the seventeenth, eighteenth, and nineteenth centuries, the vast bucolic Alhambra calling cards of the colonial cognoscenti.

Ameliorated by Hollywood's aura of moonlight and magnolias, actual plantation life was a suffocating tale of contradictory truths: Charleston's plantation class was a coterie of demagogues willing to endure isolation, tropical malaise, and the threat of slave revolts to achieve landed gentry status. And they were *au fait*, able to amass empires of wealth born from the lowly seeds of rice, indigo, and cotton. Families spent winter months sequestered away in the hinterland, so when they arrived in Charleston for the social season, life took a frenzied pitch. Starting in January with a string of balls, concerts, and sporting events that lasted until the inland threat of malaria had subsided and families could safely return to their rural homesteads, city life was an artful riot of excess.

Boone Hall
1235 Long
Point Road, Mt.
Pleasant
www.boonehall
plantation.com
(843) 884-4371

Drayton Hall
3380 Ashley River
Road
www.draytonhall
.org
(843) 766-0188

Magnolia
Plantation
3550 Ashley River
Road
www.magnolia
plantation.com
(800) 367-3517

Middleton
Plantation
4300 Ashley River
Road
www.middleton
place.org
(843) 556-6020

Of the more than 300 known plantations that at one time existed in Charleston County, almost all have been erased by time. Fortunately, four sterling examples, each with varied personality, are accessible to the public.

Boone Hall, with its parading allée of grand oaks, best satisfies the visitor searching for Scarlett's silver-screen Tara and is the only historic plantation with a working farm that still sells seasonal vegetables. The austere grandeur of Drayton Hall, void of electricity or running water, is a pinnacle example of Georgian Palladian architecture. The appropriately named Magnolia boasts a profusion of colorful flora. Its groves of azaleas and camellias are among the largest collections in the nation. Although the main house is long gone, one of North America's best examples of a Colonial garden exists at Middleton, where visitors can stroll through the sixty-five acres of parterres and verdant terraces that took ten years to create, yet thrive unto this day.

OYSTER ROAST

Salty, slurpy, and quick to slide down your throat, oysters are not only a favorite Lowcountry food, they're a social institution, and they're not for the faint of heart. Author Jonathan Swift purportedly said of the curious mollusk, "He was a bold man that first ate an oyster," and anyone who remembers his or her first oyster foray is likely to agree.

Charlestonians so love the rumored aphrodisiac with its briny perfume and succulent meat, they host an entire festival in its honor. Every January, thousands of enthusiastic shuckers converge upon Boone Hall, where two tractor trailers full of the shelled morsels tally up to the World's Largest Oyster Roast. Throughout the rest of the year, roasts typically coincide with marital engagements, housewarming affairs, and New Year's Eve.

The art of steaming, so that the bivalve cracks open, allowing hungry folks to pry open the thick, calcified shell with a blunt-tipped oyster knife, is a time-honored backyard tradition. Start by cornicing a low fire with cinderblocks upon which

Steam your own:
Crosby's Seafood
382 Spring Street
(843) 937-0029

Let someone else do the work:
Bowens Island
1870 Bowens
Island Road
www.bowens
islandrestaurant
.com
(843) 795-2757

Enjoy them with 10,000 of your closest friends:
www.charleston
restaurant
association.com

should rest a large sheet of griddlelike metal. Shovel a layer of oysters on the hot metal and shroud the shells in a wet burlap croaker sack. Wait five to ten minutes; listen for the popping sound and stand clear as the adductor muscle clamping the shell shut gives way.

Hard-core oyster eaters garnish the contents with little more than lemon juice, although festive gatherings are likely to offer more options, including cocktail sauce, shallot vinegar, or a custom mignonette.

If you're tight on time or backyard space, head to Bowens Island, the graffiti-strewn oyster shack that has been owned and operated by the same family since 1946. As Bowens Island celebrated its sixtieth anniversary in 2006, two pivotal events occurred: Owner Robert Barber accepted a James Beard Award naming the restaurant an American Classic, and five months later the local institution was devastated by fire. The family rallied and rebuilt the rustic restaurant, which is back to dishing up fresh-from-the-creek oysters.

RHETT BUTLER

He was dashing. He was an utter rapscallion. He stole the wind from Scarlett's haughty sails. And he was total fiction. Or was he? Enigmatically described as "a visitor from Charleston" in the opening pages of Margaret Mitchell's Pulitzer Prize–winning southern tome *Gone with the Wind,* the swashbuckling Rhett Butler character was forever immortalized in local lore when he—tired of Scarlett's insipid high jinks and her minx heart—declared, "I'm going back to Charleston, back where I belong."

With mordant wit and heart aflame for the wild southern lass who refused to be tamed, Rhett Butler personified the passion of the nouveau monde gentleman. While he adroitly navigated the depressed and dangerous wartime south, he was no match for Scarlett's come-hither moue, and their tempestuous union is considered one of the greatest love stories of American literature.

Mitchell claimed Butler to be complete fiction, but some historians believe he was inspired by the real-life Charlestonian George Alfred Trenholm, a shipping magnate turned blockade runner who profiteered off the Civil War and found himself as the improbable treasurer of the Confederacy—no small feat for a man who was reported to be on the verge of bankruptcy prior to the war. Trenholm fled to Richmond, Virginia, less than one year after his appointment, and he was imprisoned on the charges that he'd stolen Confederate gold—much like the rumors of war profiteering that ensnared Rhett Butler.

Whether Mitchell's work was a revisionist version of Trenholm's life or creation of the archetypal southern boulevardier is moot; the "charm and grace" that Rhett returned to Charleston in search of is alive and well.

COURTLY MANNERS

Courtly manners imported from England. Social rituals steeped in landed gentry traditions. Charleston's prosperity, benevolent societies, balls, and complex courtship dictated a protocol regimen unlike any other settlement in the new world. In a city where *savoir faire* is the lynchpin of her charm, Charleston's customs and reputation for impeccable decorum have long been prized as some of her best attributes. This legacy of pleasantries has parlayed into white-glove expectations for visitors and locals alike, and the city does not disappoint according to the authoritative tally of national couth.

Far from the cotillion lessons and charm schools that helped shape Charleston's aura of good breeding, Marjabelle Young Stewart (*né* Marjabelle Ruby Bryant) was born in Council Bluffs, Iowa, and delivered to an orphanage when her divorced parents could no longer tender care for their three young daughters. She ascended through the ranks of Washington, D.C.'s

Charleston School of Protocol and Etiquette www.charleston schoolofprotocol .com

society milieu by becoming an etiquette expert who counted the daughters of American presidents among her clients. Marjabelle espoused social graces to the young women of the nation's capital for two decades before a new husband took her to the Midwest, where she founded a series of etiquette classes for children, penned several books, and eventually began appraising the graciousness of American cities.

Charleston appeared on Stewart's inaugural "Best-Mannered" city list in 1977 and every year thereafter, earning the coveted top spot for eleven consecutive years until Stewart's death in 2007, upon which Charleston was awarded a lifetime achievement nod. With the Stewart family's blessing, the honor of conducting the annual Most Mannerly City contest was bestowed upon the Charleston School of Protocol and Etiquette, which continues the tradition of calculating cities' civility and announcing the voting results of the annual contest.

PINEAPPLE

Imported, cultivated, and adopted by Charlestonians, the pineapple enjoys a commission of honor as the symbol of hospitality across the Lowcountry. Renowned for being rarefied, the fruit, which interestingly mirrors a miniature palmetto tree, leapt from its starring role as the table centerpiece and wove itself into the ornamental fabric of the city, appearing as elaborate fence finials, flourishes carved in marble mantles, and decorations sculpted into doorway lintels. The home at 14 Legare, one of the city's premier examples of a single home, is the best place to catch a glimpse of the piquant fruit: It's prominently featured on the home's gate.

As one of the luminaries of the Charleston Renaissance, Elizabeth O'Neill Verner skillfully conveyed the quiet charm of her native city onto plates of metal, and her etching of the pineapple gates found at 14 Legare is among her most popular work. Behind many of the veneers captured by Verner were hidden gardens, where pineapples

Waterfront Park
34 Prioleau
Street

grew alongside Japanese plums, roses propagated from Puerto Rico, and kitchen herbs.

One of the city's largest pineapples wards over its own eight-acre garden, yet it needs no watering. In 1990 a large sculptural fountain depicting Charleston's hospitality emblem was installed in Waterfront Park, a favorite strolling grounds on the Cooper River side of the city. In that same vein, the local hospitality industry annually bestows the Golden Pineapple upon individuals who've demonstrated exceptional leadership in the tourism sector.

If its strange visage doesn't pique your interest, perhaps another iteration of the pineapple will beguile you. Charleston Light Dragoon Punch is a wicked concoction of grenadine, green tea, cherries, pineapple, oranges, lemons, whiskey, rum, Curacao, and carbonated water that is adorned with slices of the yellow darling of the tropics. Be forewarned: It takes four days to prepare and just as long to recover.

HISTORIC HOMES AND GARDENS

An invitation to peek inside some of the city's most illustrious dwellings without ogling through the garden gate makes the annual tours of historic homes a must for preservationists, horticulturalists, designers, and inquisitive folks who merely want to wander through the grandeur of old Charleston.

The festivals canvas the gamut of Charleston's aesthete architecture, including resplendent harborside mansions, French Quarter pied-à-terres, South of Broad single homes, and reclaimed cotton warehouses; but each individual tour centers on a specific downtown neighborhood, allowing guests to meander from one adjacent home to the next at a comfortable pace. Docents share short biographies of each home's lineage, including a provenance of key furnishings, before inviting guests to enjoy a self-guided tour through stately drawing rooms, detached kitchen houses–turned–guest quarters, hidden cupolas, and more.

An up-close look at family heirlooms—a cypress cabinet credited to prodigious Charleston furniture-maker

Preservation Society of Charleston
147 King Street
www.preservation society.org
(843) 722-4630

Historic Charleston Foundation
40 East Bay Street
www.historic charleston.org
(843) 723-1623

Thomas Elfe, a painting by nineteenth-century American artist Thomas Sully, a silver rice spoon from a great-great-grandmother's dowry, or perhaps a rice bed handed down through the generations—every home yields its own trove of interesting treasures, refined and homespun alike.

When the summer heat subsides, the Preservation Society of Charleston holds its fall Candlelight Tour of Homes, and when the confection-colored pink-and-white azaleas bloom, locals know it's time for Historic Charleston Foundation's annual spring tour of homes and gardens. The latter began in 1948 and attracted more than 3,000 people from thirty-eight states as a result of the first-ever concerted effort to market Charleston as a tourist destination. A subsequent article in *Antiques* magazine cemented the tours' popularity by heralding the unique peek behind typically closed doors as a way to observe how people "live with antiques which have not been collected but have been inherited from the ancestors who acquired them when they were new."

RICE SPOON

Gilded china, porcelain tureens, and sterling epergnes engraved with the family crest were the keys to executing the carefully orchestrated entertaining rituals of yesteryear. Amid the pantheon of resplendent heirloom table settings that adorn many modern downtown homes, one peculiar-looking piece of flatware stands out: the ancestral rice spoon. A long spindle, often measuring more than a foot in length, the rice spoon is the local evolution of the English stuffing spoon, the nimble extractor of delicacies cooked inside game dishes.

Colonists yearned to increase their caches of silver during the economic boom of the eighteenth century, and artful skill turned tradesmen into tycoons. The most noted silversmith of this era was Alexander Petrie who rewrote his fate as an anonymous immigrant by peddling his silver wares to eager Charlestonians. He amassed such a fortune with his Broad Street shop that he ascended to the ranks of the plantation families for whom he

*Charleston Museum
360 Meeting Street
www.charleston museum.org
(843) 722-2996*

*Croghan's Jewel Box
308 King Street
(843) 723-6589*

fulfilled commissions. Petrie's sons were educated in England, and they returned to Charleston as first-generation gentlemen. His legacy endures: A circa-1760 silver spoon marked with Petrie's sign sold for $6,875 at a Christie's auction in 2009.

One of Petrie's most interesting objects, a marrow scoop, is housed among the vast troves of Colonial silver, which includes scores of rice spoons, on

display in the Charleston Museum's permanent collection. The elongated scoop features a gully groove in its narrow handle that offers the user two ends from which to extract the shank's contents.

The spoons don't merely exist as relics preserved under glass by cultural institutions. Modern renditions of the rice spoon are a tradition-steeped wedding gift sold by several stores, most notable of which is Croghan's Jewel Box, the family-owned repository of estate pieces that has operated from King Street since 1919.

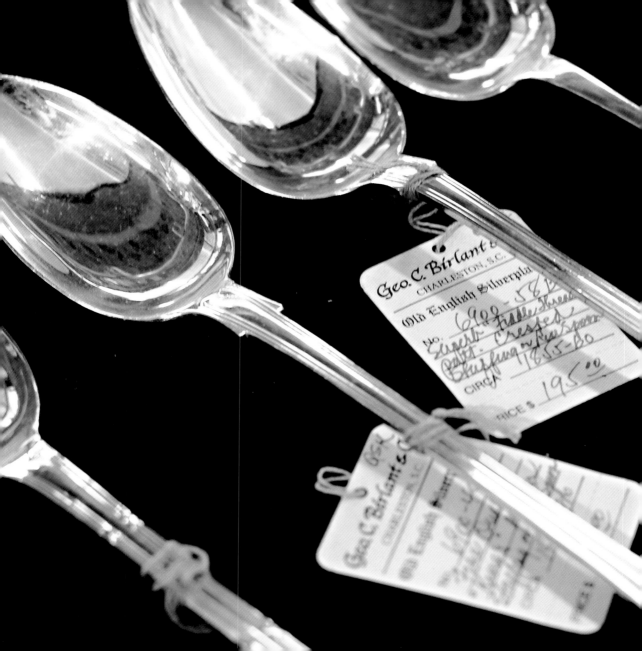

Geo. C. Birlant &
CHARLESTON, S.C.

Old English Silverpla

No. 6900 - 58

Superb Fiddle Thread

Patt. Cressed

Stuffing or Pie Spoon

CIRCA 1855-80

195 00

PRICE $

PHILIP SIMMONS GATES

Binding soulless metal to a lush cultural identity, pastoral elements drawn from a barrier island rearing, is the hallmark of Charleston's most prodigious blacksmith, Philip Simmons.

Raised near the rushes of Daniel Island and schooled in the ways of a Sea Island fisherman, young Simmons was ferried over to Charleston at age eight to begin a proper education. For someone who'd never seen paved roads or buildings other than simple, clapboard dwellings, the cacophonous discovery of men beating and bending hot iron, which he happened upon while walking home from Buist Academy one day, left Simmons awestruck. From that point on, he was schooled amid a shower of sparks by tutors at the smithy.

Simmons first shod horses and repaired carriages, then tried his hand at reconditioning the ironwork adorning homes when the advent of the automo-

*Philip Simmons
Foundation
www.philip
simmons.us*

bile rendered the wagon archaic. It was a fortuitous evolution in technology for this old-world craftsman. His skill for ornamental work soon became apparent and a beautiful legacy was born: Simmons's vigorous physical labor, melded with the powerful influence of his natural surroundings, transmuted cold, stark raw material into a graceful art form.

Today, the city is festooned with hundreds of Simmons's gates, each uniquely imbued with honeycombed curlicues and indigenous snakes, birds, and fish. No other artisan has left so widespread a mark on Charleston. The oeuvre of Simmons's blacksmithery helped cement his place as a venerated artisan and not just a laborer. His ability to fuse a time-honored technique with contemporary aesthetic earned his work a place in the Smithsonian Museum, for which he created a gate showcasing a Daniel Island spottail bass.

SHRIMP BOATS

Flying Cloud, Winds of Fortune, Carolina, Lady Eva, and *Anna Grace.* The alluring names obscure the gritty nature of the oil-smudged trawlers that prowl local waters on the hunt for seafood bounty. Roused before daybreak, the small but mighty fleet kisses the aurora sky as it chugs out of sheltered moorings, like the one at Shem Creek, and heads toward open waters for a long day of honest work.

Shrimp stay close to shore, so the boats—green-winged, diesel-powered dinosaurs that can measure up to eighty-five feet in length—run parallel to the coast in a sight that is as familiar to inhabitants of Maine as the lobster trapper.

Many captains, sea salts who often inherited the job from a father or uncle, track the shrimp by instinct—wisdom of the running tides and estuary spawning grounds ingrained by a rich maritime heritage; however, the use of GPS and sonar have become the time-saving arsenal against foreign competition that threatens to eradicate the local industry.

Blessing
of the Fleet
www.townof
mountpleasant
.com

In 2004 a Charleston-based initiative called Wild American Shrimp launched a compelling campaign that encouraged people to buy locally sourced seafood, and it successfully heightened awareness of the Lowcountry shrimpers' plight. Despite the adverse ecological and economical impact of foreign, farm-raised shrimp, the simple matter is that the wild American variety caught in the waters off the coast of southeastern states are more flavorful and lower in cholesterol. A more recent hurdle, escalating fuel costs, means boats must bank 300 pounds of the pink crustaceans per day in order to break even, which is backbreaking work on a good day and desolation when conditions are awry.

But shrimpers are a hardy bunch and the community embraces their dedication to an arcane profession. For more than two decades, the town of Mt. Pleasant has held a preseason ceremonial blessing of the fleet that solicits a benison of safety and prosperity for every trawler and her crew.

SHRIMP AND GRITS

Rivulets of rich, dense gravy; sweet, white shrimp hauled from a local creek by hand with a seine; slow-cooked stone-ground grits that require constant, methodical stirring; and the occasional leftover—like a ham hock—from the previous night's dinner, shrimp and grits began as a rustic, hearty breakfast that capitalized on abundant local ingredients but has transcended its humble beginnings to become the savory workhorse of many local menus.

Scores of restaurants feature the quintessential meal as a lunch or dinner entrée (in addition, of course, to breakfast fare), and nuanced variations span the city. At Fleet Landing, the casual, family-friendly restaurant housed on a pier that juts onto the harbor, the recipe calls for jumbo shrimp and andouille sausage in a shellfish glaze over creamy grits with fresh scallions. A block west at

Fleet Landing
186 Concord
Street
www.fleetlanding
.net
(843) 722-8100

Slightly
North of Broad
192 East Bay
Street
www.maverick
southernkitchens
.com
(843) 723-3424

Hominy Grill
207 Rutledge
Avenue
www.hominygrill
.com
(843) 937-0930

Slightly North of Broad, the de facto lunch stop for local business folk, Chef Frank Lee serves up local yellow grits with shrimp, housemade sausage, country ham, tomatoes, and green onions. Across town at Hominy Grill, the immediately recognizable salmon-hued building with its marquee depicting a woman holding a bowl of grits, Chef Robert Stehling (named best chef in the southeast by the James Beard Foundation in 2008) sautés shrimp with scallions, mushrooms, and bacon, which he serves over cheese grits.

Purists use little more than grits, milk, shrimp, and butter, but other recipes call for sharp cheddar cheese, Tabasco, truffles, or white wine. Some instruct that grits should be cooked in a double broiler; one suggests a Crock-Pot. There's even an entire cookbook that waxes poetic about the dish!

MORRIS ISLAND LIGHTHOUSE

When colonists decided to erect the first man-made light to probe the coastal waters off Charles Towne, they selected Morris Island, a windswept spit of land at the mouth of the harbor, to house the navigational beacon. The year was 1673, and the fledgling three-year-old settlement was well on its way to becoming a "great port towne," a destiny predicted by Carolina land baron Lord Proprietor Anthony Ashley Cooper. The rudimentary pitch and oakum pyre illuminated the darkness for ships and tolerance-seeking émigrés alike—two entwining tenets of Charleston's formative history.

Hurricanes, earthquakes, wars, and a thriving merchant marine economy levied a toll on the neophyte light. It sustained three subsequent iterations, including a 42-foot tower erected in 1767; a 102-foot tower, circa 1838; and a 150-foot tower, circa 1876.

Ultimately, it was an act of man that forever changed the fate of the lighthouse. In 1889, an extensive pair

Save the Light, Inc.
www.savethe
light.org

of parallel jetties—the magnitude of which had never been seen in the United States—were installed to protect the depth and flow of the heavily trafficked shipping channel. The intended impact was achieved, but the project also caused an unforeseen implication: The current shifted and large portions of Morris Island eroded into the sea.

As the waves continued to siphon off the sands surrounding the lighthouse, plans for a new, higher ground tower were put forth. In 1963 the brilliant beam that served for so many years as the metronome of Charleston's bustling maritime economy was extinguished.

In 2007 the Army Corps of Engineers spearheaded work to gird the structural stability of the then-131-year-old tower and not a moment too soon. The shoreline has receded several hundred feet, leaving the lighthouse an island unto itself amid the undulating ocean. Though she still stands proud, she gently genuflects toward the sea due to her crumbling foundation.

HOLY CITY SKYLINE

It's speckled with spires: dramatic silhouettes that pierce a blazing sunset, symbols of resistance and renewal. While European monarchs waged oppressive, bloody battles over the salvation of the hoi polloi, residents of Charles Towne adopted a transcendental egalitarianism toward the religions of fellow colonists as evidenced by the church steeples that tower over the city. Early inhabitants subscribed to Christianity and Judaism, congregating as members of the Anglican, Calvinist, Huguenot, Lutheran, Methodist, Presbyterian, Reformist, Quaker, and Unitarian faiths.

By the 1760s, six permanent houses of worship had been erected. During the American Revolution, wily colonists coated their church steeples with black paint to render them invisible against the night sky and thus protected from the bombardments of British warships. After fleeing religious persecution and surviving the arduous ocean passage, Charlestonians had little tolerance for a threat against their freedom to worship. Today, Charleston is an exemplar of

St. Michael's Church 71 Broad Street

religious harmony with more than 400 churches populating the city.

The melodious peal of bells, a luminous call-to-worship, call-to-matrimony, or call-to-mourn evocation that spreads across the city like honeyed psalms, is an oft-heard sound. Perhaps no other bells are as sonorous or storied as those belonging to the paragon of early churches: St. Michael's. Its eight bells, the largest of which weighs 1,945 pounds, were originally cast in London in 1764. Less than twenty years later, they became wartime plunder when the retreating British smuggled them out of the city in the wake of the American Revolution. The bells were recovered and returned to the congregation but confiscated on the eve of the Civil War with the intention of being recast as artillery. The chimes were saved from a fate as cannonballs, but the misshapen metal had to be sent back to the original foundry to be recast. They went back to London for the third and final time following Hurricane Hugo and have been regaling the city ever since.

STREET NAMES

A map of the city reveals a rich narrative that hints at the individuals who contributed to the blueprint of the peninsula, personalities whose destinies shaped Charleston. The tradition of ennobling British lords by christening streets in their honor is best evidenced by George, Anson, Scarborough, and Bowling Green streets, named for Lord of the Admiralty George Anson, one of his ships, and his plantation, respectively. The city itself—Charles Towne—beatified King Charles.

Appointed officials were duly added to the annals of history when their last names appeared on the city grid. Such men included John Archdale, a staunch advocate of tolerance who served as governor; Lord Charles Greville Montague, the last colonial governor of South Carolina; General Christopher Gadsden, lieutenant governor during the American Revolution; William Bull, the last royally appointed lieutenant governor; and Robert Hayne, the first mayor of Charles Towne. The men did not possess a monopoly on name veneration. Ann, Gadsden's wife,

Maps available at the Charleston Visitor Center 375 Meeting Street

leant her first name to the Wraggsborough neighborhood, while a street named for her sister, Elizabeth, exists one block away.

At the apogee of the plantation era, an age marked by astounding wealth and ensuing opulence, the streets were paved with gold for the upper echelon of Charlestonians who bound their storied names to the growing city. Arnold Vanderhorst (pronounced Van-dross), a prominent landholder whose deeds included 2,350 acres on Kiawah and a city wharf, put his stamp on a street that today winds its way past the College of Charleston and Ashley Hall school for girls. Nearby, one of the city's primary east-west arteries, Calhoun Street, borrows its name from two-term vice president John C. Calhoun, whose landholdings later became Clemson University.

One of the best places to start a walking tour of the city is Tradd Street, the shaded South of Broad thoroughfare heavily weighted with stately single homes that was reportedly named in honor of the first child born in the city, Robert Tradd, in 1679.

PRESERVATION SOCIETIES

The fates of fortune have toyed with Charleston, thrusting her into the echelon of rarefied wealth and casting her into postwar decrepitude, but even when residents were "too poor to paint, too proud to whitewash," Charlestonians ardently protected their vaulted, although sometimes shabby, homes. The population migration of the early twentieth century, however, introduced a dilemma: As people moved west, homes with historic merit sat vacant, falling into a dilapidated state. Who would tender care?

Born from the pressing need for stewardship, the oldest community-based historic preservation organization in the United States was founded in Charleston in 1920 when the fledgling Society for the Preservation of Old Dwellings took up the charge to rescue the then 118-year-old Joseph Manigault House, an exemplary Federal-style structure. Eleven years later, the society influenced city council to adopt what would alter the face of Charleston forever: the first zoning ordinance intended to protect historic

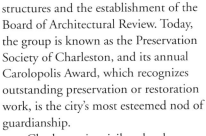

Preservation Society of Charleston
147 King Street
www.preservation society.org
(843) 722-4630

Historic Charleston Foundation
40 East Bay Street
www.historic charleston.org
(843) 723-1623

structures and the establishment of the Board of Architectural Review. Today, the group is known as the Preservation Society of Charleston, and its annual Carolopolis Award, which recognizes outstanding preservation or restoration work, is the city's most esteemed nod of guardianship.

Charleston is privileged to have two preservation-minded organizations dedicated to protecting the historical and architectural vestiges of the city through advocacy and conservation. In 1947 Historic Charleston Foundation (HCF) was incorporated as a nonprofit with an eye toward urban renewal. HCF established the nation's first fund for the rehabilitation of entire city blocks and set about buying threatened properties, overseeing restoration, selling to preservation-minded buyers, and reinvesting in the next dilapidated neighborhood. With the use of easements, the foundation asserted maintenance of restored buildings in perpetuity, and the merits of that early work are seen across the peninsula.

RAINBOW ROW

A collection of connected masonry dwellings that housed the merchants who peddled wares at the nearby wharves, the thirteen frequently photographed homes of 79–107 East Bay Street are an indelible part of Charleston's urbanscape.

Although Philadelphia is most closely associated with row houses thanks to its mid–eighteenth century Elfreth's Alley, Charleston's early row homes also date to that era, but the first structures were eradicated by fire in 1740. Subsequent homes were ravaged by shelling during the American Revolution and then left to crumble in the wake of the Civil War. By the 1920s the dilapidated tenements had so distressed city council that a motion to demolish and redevelop the block was put forth. Fortunately, hints at an uptick in the economy, optimism beyond the Depression, and a burgeoning cultural renaissance allayed such a drastic action.

In 1932 Dorothy Porcher Legge seized upon an idea to enhance the sur-

Rainbow Row 79–107 East Bay Street

83-107 EAST BAY STREET
RAINBOW ROW

Rainbow Row represents the longest cluster of intact Georgian row houses in the United States. The earliest structures on this portion of East Bay Street, between Tradd and Elliott Street, were built by 1680. The buildings were constructed on lots 7 to 10 of the Grand Modell, a city plan developed between 1670-1680.

Over the years, the buildings served as the shops and residences of notable merchants and planters, and fronted a cluster of wharves on the Cooper River waterfront. The buildings also fronted a segment of the eastern boundary of the fortification wall constructed circa 1704 to surround the city. Some of the houses were damaged or destroyed by fire, and the present structures date from circa 1720 to circa 1790. The homes suffered slight damage by Union artillery bombardment during the War between the States.

face vanity of the street: fresh paint in a variety of Caribbean colors. The first home to get a pastel-hued facelift belonged to Legge and her husband, Lionel, who festooned their residence at 99–101 East Bay with a shocking shade of pink.

Legge joined forces with the city's vanguard preservationist, Susan Frost Pringle, who founded the Preservation for Historic Dwellings more than a decade earlier. Together, they outlined a scope of acquisition, restoration, and profit—Pringle was, after all, the city's first female real estate agent. It was their hope that revitalization of East Bay would spread to Tradd Street, another one of Pringle's pet projects, and thus raise awareness of preservation throughout the Lower Peninsula.

Other colors bloomed, including blue and yellow, and Rainbow Row, the colloquial name for the whimsically colored homes entered Charleston vernacular.

FORTS

Profiteering European seadogs, plundering pirates, the power-hungry English crown, and eventually her own federal government—a ceaseless stream of would-be usurpers assailed Charleston's coast for more than a century after the colony's founding in 1670. The city's proximity to the open ocean left her vulnerable to attack, a weakness that local leaders sought to stem by garrisoning the harbor. The defense network, comprised of four forts, took 125 years to complete and began in 1704 with Fort Johnson. Although it remained largely on the periphery of the city's skirmishes, it hosted one particularly noteworthy event: The crescent moon flag, the forerunner of the current state flag, was first hoisted at this location.

The only tweak to that first flag, the addition of the palmetto tree, is credited to the second fort added to Charleston's growing constellation of citadels. Construction of a garrison located on Sullivan's Island was under way when nine

Fort Moultrie
www.nps.gov/
fomo

Fort Sumter
www.nps.gov/
fosu

British warships attacked in 1776. Built with soft, pliable palmetto logs that absorbed the impact of cannonballs, the fort helped successfully defend Charleston in the early surges of the American Revolution. The pivotal victory galvanized the freedom fighters' commitment to the cause, momentum that led to the colonists' ability to upturn the crown's sovereign control.

Construction of Castle Pinckney began in 1797 when war with France seemed possible and colonists wanted to stave off naval attacks, but this small brick bastion saw more action as a powder magazine and prison.

In 1829, a shoal at the mouth of the harbor was fortified with granite and designated as a site for the fourth garrison, Fort Sumter. The most expansive of all the forts, it was designed to house hundreds of soldiers and more than 100 heavy artillery guns. In addition to its dominant size, Fort Sumter's role in history looms as the starting place of the Civil War.

THE CITADEL

The clap of a booming cannon breeches the tranquility of the Upper Peninsula most Friday afternoons during the academic year. That's when the Citadel's Corps of Cadets marches across Summerall Field in a dazzling display of spit polish and precision much to the delight of family members, friends, and curious onlookers. Although the fortresslike military college may appear closed to the outside world, the public is welcome to watch the weekly pageantry per the schedule posted on the school's Web site.

Since its founding in 1842, the Citadel has educated future Fulbright scholars, governors, congressmen, scores of military heroes, and celebrated native son Pat Conroy, whose 1980 novel *The Lords of Discipline* detailed a fictional account of ruthless cadet hazing. Indeed, freshmen students, known as knobs, are subject to rigorous immersion in mili-

*The Citadel
171 Moultrie
Street
www.citadel.edu
(843) 225-3294*

taristic rituals—frequent inspections, arduous twice-daily physical-fitness regimens, weapons drills, and long hours spent standing in formation.

Although not all graduates commit to military service, cadets have played several storied roles throughout history, from the school's creation as a municipal guard charged with maintaining public order in Charleston, to its students firing the first shot in the Civil War, and the entire class of 1944 being drafted into armed service during World War II.

In the midst of the school's gray, imposing twenty-seven-building compound is a solemn bastion of grace and reverence: the nondenominational, fourteenth-century Gothic-style Summerall Chapel. Every December, cadets representing numerous faiths join their voices for a stirring advent concert, to which the public is also invited.

HUNLEY SUBMARINE

On August 8, 2000, a flotilla of powerboats signaled an air horn fanfare as a barely recognizable, barnacle-encrusted submarine breeched the surface of the waters off Charleston for the first time in more than 136 years. Retrieved from the ocean floor by a crane-operated harness and a salvage barge teeming with scientists, the *H. L. Hunley* was the prize in a modern-day treasure hunt that had eluded historians, researchers, and novelists for decades.

The American Civil War gave rise to an era of furious invention, and with the blockaded Charleston harbor strangling the ability to resupply Confederate troops, a creative strategy was needed to usurp the Union forces.

Harnessing the power of ballast tanks, the world's first successful sub-

Friends of the
Hunley
www.hunley.org

marine—a warfare chimera that sluiced through the water rather than riding atop the waves, giving it the element of surprise when launched under the cloak of night—represented a quantum leap in naval warfare.

In the eerie suba-quatic environment, the only sounds were the metal grind of the crank-shaft and the breath of the crew who were motor-ing into both the history books and, unbeknownst to them, a watery grave. Their objective? Ram the enemy ship with the torpedo spar, which they successfully accomplished on January 17, 1864, resulting in the sinking of the USS *Housatonic*. What happened next is lost to obscurity, but a team of forensic scientists at the Warren Lasch Conservation Lab con-tinues to study the artifacts and piece together the story.

BEACHES AND BARRIER ISLANDS

The pearl-gray, weathered bark of the skeletal, sea-swept trees marooned in the arboreal graveyards on Charleston's barrier islands shines like abalone. Lashed by wind and water, the archipelago that snakes along the coastal plain is a haven for naturalists and a photographer's nirvana. Although Capers, Bull, and Morris Islands are uninhabited, the ecosystems are teeming with life. The leeward salt marsh estuaries nurture maritime microcosms full of scuttling crabs, playful dolphins, breaching trout, popping oyster beds, and the occasional wily alligator. Eagles, herons, pelicans,

Capers Island
www.dnr.sc.gov

Ferry to Bull
Island
www.coastal
expeditions.com

Dewees Island
www.dewees
islandpoa.org

Isle of Palms
www.iop.net

Sullivan's Island
www.sullivans
island-sc.com

Folly Beach
www.cityoffolly
beach.com

Kiawah Island
www.kiawah
resort.com

Seabrook Island
www.discover
seabrook.com

and ospreys delight the most ardent birdwatchers. Turtle hatchlings rushing toward the sea under a silvery moonlit sky is one of the Lowcountry's most magical natural events.

Scarcely populated during Charleston's early history save for forts, quarantines, and lighthouses, the area turned into a homebuilding juggernaut in the 1970s as people flocked to the seabreeze lifestyle. Dewees, however, is an excellent example of conscientious development: Sixty-three percent of the island remains in its natural state, island roads remain unpaved, and boardwalks protect the dunes while providing access to the pristine beach.

With ninety miles of beaches and a temperate year-round climate, the coast is a constant hub of activity. Most people arrive in Charleston with an eye toward swimming, sunbathing, and sand-castle building. There's a beach for everyone: Both Kiawah's and Seabrook's beaches are quietly private, funky Folly has the best waves for surfers, the sands of Sullivan's Island are family-friendly, and Isle of Palms is a party waiting for the sun to set.

GOLF

A mere thirty-six years after the founding of the Royal and Ancient Golf Club of St. Andrews in 1786, one of the world's oldest and most venerated courses, Scottish émigrés imported the curious game of clubs and caddies from their native misty moors to Charleston's sandy shores. Harleston Green, the first golf course and club to be founded in North America, lasted less than fifteen years at its location on the outskirts of town, but it foretold the great legacy of golf that dominates the region today. A novel anomaly amid the sporting set's ardor for horse racing and hunts, golf endured. By the 1920s Bermuda grass greens were cropping up across the Lowcountry, which led to the eventual realization that wild tangle of marshland forest and undulating sand dune topography was an ideally challenging landscape for games of golf.

It was Tom Fazio's Links Course at Wild Dunes on Isle of Palms that

Links Course
www.wilddunes
.com
(843) 886-2180

Ocean Course
www.kiawah
resort.com
(800) 576-1570

RiverTowne
www.ginnbel
videre.com
(866) 216-3777

formally piqued the interest of the golfing world. Designed in the 1970s, it dovetailed the splendor of a seaside setting with the environmental rigors of an unforgiving barrier island, and it is still considered one of the nation's top 100 courses.

Down the coast at Kiawah Island, the famously windswept Ocean Course is shrouded in mystique. This Pete Dye design earned the distinction of "America's Toughest Resort Course" by *Golf Digest,* and it bared its brio to the world during the hotly contested 1991 Ryder Cup, which became known as the "War by the Shore."

Along Mt. Pleasant's peaceful Horlbeck Creek, the Arnold Palmer–designed course at the RiverTowne Country Club received its share of national exposure in 2007 and 2008, when top-seeded Annika Sorenstam hosted an LPGA tournament with one of the largest purses in the history of women's golf.

HIGH BATTERY

The dynasty of scions lines the city's southern seawall, where a row of astonishing mansions salute the sweeping harbor in a union of style and setting that make this three-block neighborhood the apogee of local real estate.

The cache of Greek Revival–style homes includes the Desaussure House (1850), John Ravenel House (1849), Roper House (1838), William Ravenel House (1845), and the Edmonston-Alston House (1829), a museum operated by the Middleton Place Foundation that invites the public to have an up-close look at its drawing rooms adorned with late Federal and Regency style decorations.

The eye-popping homes were built on infill land sold by the city to subsidize the adjacent 6.5-acre White Point Gardens, an inviting park so named for its historic mounds of bleached oyster shells. A wide, oleander-lined promenade winds past the homes and the park making the tip of the peninsula one of

Edmonston-Alston House
4300 Ashley River Road
www.middleton place.org
(843) 556-6020

the most accessible parts of the city.

Rimming the shaded greensward are glazed cannons muted long ago but still pointing toward the harbor, guarding the city against the high-seas scalawags of yesteryear. Although this grassy preserve is perfect for picnics, pirates once swung from gallows on this spot. The "gentleman pirate" Stede Bonnet was the most notorious of all who were hanged here. He and approximately two-dozen of his crew were left to dangle and rot in the wind—a grisly greeting card to other would-be marauders. In a more honorable salute, a monument erected in celebration of the centennial anniversary of Sergeant Jasper's heroics during the American Revolution presides over the southeastern end of the park.

Charleston Battery Benches invite visitors to sit a spell, and there is no better spot from which to contemplate on the arrival of the colonists, who sailed past this very point in 1670.

CHARLESTON BATTERY BENCH

Wander past the King Street storefront of Geo. C. Birlant & Co., with its gleaming silver rice spoons lined up in the window like toy soldiers, and turn west onto Cumberland Street. Tucked into the back of the unassuming brick building is one of the city's enduring cottage industries: the workshop where the Charleston Battery Bench is fabricated.

Commissioned by the city for the purpose of beautifying Whitepoint Gardens, the park lining the tip of the peninsula, the Battery Bench was originally cast in the mid-nineteenth century by J. F. Riley Iron Works, a local company whose eclectic cadre of work also included framework for lighthouses around Key West, Florida. When production ceased, Geo. C. Birlant & Co., one of the city's largest

Geo. C. Birlant & Co.
191 King Street
www.birlant.com
(843) 722-3842

and longest-running antiques emporiums, acquired the original molds and the exclusive rights to fabricate the distinctive bench. Three generations later, they're still hard at work handcrafting benches.

The distinctive cypress slat–and–cast iron filigreed creation holds native flora and fauna secrets revealed only upon close inspection. The now-extinct Carolina parakeet, the green-and-yellow plumaged bird that disappeared soon after 1900; a fox and hound nod to the sporting set; and indigenous foliage are all woven into the pedestal and armrest frieze. Weighing in at seventy-five pounds, the four-foot bench is a hefty lawn ornament, yet the family-owned Birlant & Co. has shipped numerous orders to overseas customers.

HURRICANE HUGO

The sound of a hurricane—a thundering freight train bearing down at a deafening decibel—is unforgettable. For those who choose to ride out a big storm, it is a malevolent sound that represents a time of sheer horror.

Despite Governor Carroll Campbell's order of evacuation for low-lying coastal areas, many inhabitants of McClellanville, a sleepy fishing village due north of Charleston, gathered in the local high school–turned–Red Cross Shelter to wait out Hurricane Hugo. That night, as the storm made landfall, a twenty-foot storm tide roared ashore flooding nearby Jeremy Creek and filling the school with water. More than 500 terrified residents huddled in the dark as the battered building groaned against the wailing wind. Panic crept in as the water began to rise, and the refugees spent the night clinging to

A plaque identifying the people who died in the storm is affixed to the eastern seawall adjacent to the Battery's White Point Gardens.

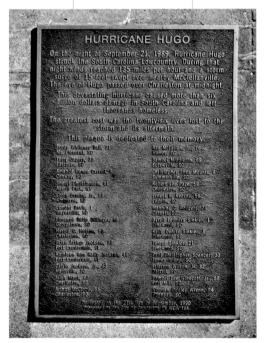

the rafters, praying for their lives. The wind, a wailing banshee, tormented them till dawn. Fortunately, everyone at the school survived the storm, but twenty people lost their lives in other parts of the state amid $7 billion in damages.

Hurricane Hugo was a classic Cape Verde hurricane that swung across the Atlantic Ocean from Africa building steam along the way. By the time it slammed into the Carolina coast on September 21, 1989, the Category 4 storm had winds of 135 miles per hour, which wreaked previously unseen levels of havoc on the coast and amounted to historic damages. It was a defining moment for Charleston, but the city emerged from the devastation as a tight-knit community with a repolished edifice and a plan to revitalize local industry.

HURRICANE HUGO

he night of September 21, 1989, Hurricane Hu
ck the South Carolina Lowcountry. During that
winds reached 135 miles per hour and a stor
ge of 15 feet swept over nearby McClellanville
eye of Hugo passed over Charleston at midnigh
is devastating hurricane caused more than six
lion dollars damage in South Carolina and left
thousands homeless.
wenty-six lives lost to th

ARTHUR RAVENEL JR. BRIDGE

The weather plays a fantastic sleight-of-hand trick in Charleston. On foggy days, the white suspension cables and foundation towers of the majestic Arthur Ravenel Jr. Bridge meld into the mist making the eight-lane causeway appear to float in the ether. Likewise on clear days, the city's apogee is hard to ignore: The concrete *arc du ciel* dominates the landscape with its two diamond-shaped towers that soar 575 feet above the sea.

The bridge opened in July 2005, one year ahead of schedule, and was heralded as a design-build architectural achievement of titanic proportions. Construction began before the schematics were complete, and spans originating from opposite sides of the Cooper River inched toward one another at an astonishing rate. Perhaps the only thing more eye-popping than the rapid assembly of the nearly 2.5-mile bridge was the opening ceremony fireworks extravaganza

Cooper River Bridge Run www.bridgerun .com

that showered the modernist structure with the sparks of 60,000 exploding rockets.

The $632 million bridge required a variety of local, state, and federal level collaborations and was named for a homespun legislator who played a pivotal role in securing funding for the project. With an investment of that magnitude, it was vital that engineers take into consideration the threat of natural disasters, namely hurricane and earthquake activity. The bridge's tensile strength is designed to withstand wind gusts in excess of 300 miles per hour and ground tremors measuring 7.4 on the Richter scale—in addition to the stampeding madness of the runners and walkers who cross the span every spring during the annual Cooper River Bridge Run, a 10-kilometer foot race that began in 1978 and attracts thousands of athletes from around the world.

EARTHQUAKE BOLTS

A curious mix of shyster sales pitch and a seemingly practical engineering solution, the earthquake bolt appeared *en masse* in late 1886 as tremor-ravaged Charlestonians frantically sought ways to salvage buildings in the aftermath of the cataclysmic earthquake that reduced a fourth of the city to rubble. The epicenter originated in the sleepy town of Summerville, some twenty-five miles inland of Charleston, and the sway, which caused church bells to ring involuntarily, was reportedly detected all along the eastern seaboard—as far away as Atlanta, Chicago, and New York City. When the shaking subsided, more than 100 people were dead and the face of the city was largely unrecognizable. Residents were reeling.

The newfangled invention that

235 Meeting Street

51 East Battery

85 East Bay Street

1 Broad Street

promised to gird dwellings with cross-width iron rods affixed to anchors bolted on exterior walls that spanned the crawl space between floors may have seemed plausible; however, the bowed masonry would have remained unstable despite the retrofit. But Charleston loves her decorative ornamentation, and it wasn't long before an array of attractive cast-iron finials, or earthquake bolt coverings, appeared on buildings across the peninsula.

Lion heads, stars, circular plates, and rectangular bars were among the more popular designs and can be seen today on a number of downtown residences, including 235 Meeting Street (lion heads), 51 East Battery (stars), 85 East Bay (circular), and 1 Broad Street (bars).

BOILED PEANUTS

Don't be surprised to see I BRAKE FOR BOILED PEANUTS pronounced on the bumper of a car crisscrossing the peninsula. It's a cheeky wink at the state's official snack, a roadside-stand delicacy that is one of Charleston's most bizarre—and revered—food items. The quip, popularized by *The Lee Bros. Boiled Peanuts Catalogue,* a mail-order smorgasbord of southern fare founded by a pair of native sons, encapsulates the zeal with which people in Charleston hunt their boiled peanuts.

Harvested in a green state, fresh from the ground and full of moisture, raw peanuts are plunged into a boiling salt bath for at least an hour. The brining process softens the shell, rendering the nut a velvety texture, but don't dare ever call the contents mushy!

Aficionados are divided between two eating methods: One faction pops the nut—wrinkly, salt-drenched shells and all—into the mouth for a satisfying suckle, while the other side cracks each nut open like an oyster and slurps out the contents. The only real requisite is a place to dis-

Lee Bros.
Boiled Peanuts
Catalogue
www.boiled
peanuts.com
(843) 720-8890

Tony the
Peanut Man
www.tonypeanut
man.com
(843) 793-4900

card the wet shells.

Peanuts first appeared in the Lowcountry with the arrival of the West African slave trade in the seventeenth century, although the origin of the boiled preparation is unknown. Written accounts from the Civil War front line mention boiling peanuts, a surprisingly nutrient-rich legume, to supplant the lack of bread or meat. Since then, the unassuming goober has become the recipient of gourmet dressing. Some boilers imbue the stewpot with ham hock or Cajun seasonings to infuse the peanut with added zest.

If the stewed style of peanuts doesn't suit your palate, perhaps the more pedestrian preparation of roasting will satisfy your craving for the salty snack. Wearing a porkpie hat fashioned from sweetgrass reeds and shouting his catchy jingle, *"Got some boiled, got some roasted, got some stewed, got some toasted,"* Tony the Peanut Man is a colorful character who peddles mostly roasted goobers at parades, festivals, sporting events, and the city market.

FOUR CORNERS OF LAW

The fast-and-louche denizens of the wharves, transient sailors looking for grog, companionship, and streets to carouse, clamored out of control soon after the city's founding, forcing the governor to mandate tavern licensing in 1669, an effort to vanquish the illicit "disorderly houses" that distracted laborers and mariners and caused "neglect of their Trades and services." A subsequent act in 1680 called for "the suppression of Idle, Drunken and Swearing Persons." This clash between Charles Towne's taint of frontier lawless and old-world civility demanded that the fledgling city assert itself. Enforcement was the charge of the governor's proxy—constables and churchwardens—a partnership that portended the city's evolution of morality.

Divine law was the first to establish a foundation at the city's crossroads of rectitude. In 1752, the cornerstone of St. Michael's, the city's oldest church, was laid at the southeast corner of Broad and Meeting streets. The following year, a building intended to seat

St. Michael's
Church
71 Broad Street

Charleston
City Hall
80 Broad Street

Charleston
County
Courthouse
82 Broad Street

United States
Post Office
83 Broad Street

the provincial capital of the colony was erected on the corner diagonally west of the church. Construction of city hall, on the corner due north of the church, occurred in 1800. Nearly 100 years later, the four-way convergence of law—ecclesiastical, state, local, and federal—was complete when the U.S. Post Office opened on the corner due east of the church.

The four buildings illustrate the intricate local architecture. The wide portico and towering steeple of St. Michael's are reminiscent of English churches from the eighteenth century. The original statehouse, which burned during the Constitutional Ratification Convention of 1788, was replaced by a neoclassical design in 1792 and today houses the county courthouse. The Adamesque style of city hall is attributed to architect Gabriel Manigault. The most ornate of the four, the Renaissance Revival–style post office, is embellished with quoins and parapet balconies cut from gray granite.

LIVABILITY COURT

The New York Times, 48 Hours, and mayors across the country have taken note: In Charleston, quality of life issues are handled in succinct fashion by a novel institution called the Livability Court. It's not surprising that a city known for its manners and gracious inhabitants would start the country's first court dedicated solely to mediating local disputes such as barking dogs and unkempt yards. According to presiding Judge Michael Molony, who helped found the court in 2002 along with oft-lauded visionary Mayor Joseph P. Riley Jr., the court has become a successful forum to deal with issues unique to Charleston, a city founded in 1670 and ill-equipped to address modern pressures of city life, including tourists, a growing college student body, restaurants, traffic, pollution, and noise.

Without costing the city any additional money, Riley and Molony devised a way of diverting neighborly disputes that previously bogged down the case-laden municipal court system. Biweekly,

**Livability Court
180 Lockwood
Boulevard**

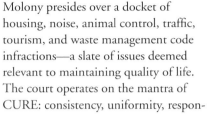

Molony presides over a docket of housing, noise, animal control, traffic, tourism, and waste management code infractions—a slate of issues deemed relevant to maintaining quality of life. The court operates on the mantra of CURE: consistency, uniformity, responsiveness, and enforcement. Once Molony interprets the law and hands down a judgment, the court's two full-time officers ensure prompt execution of the ruling.

Prior to the Livability Court, regulatory agencies like the Board of Architectural Review had little recourse to enforce ordinance violations, but the court, which corrals department heads from various city offices, has the resources to get problems resolved—immediately.

While the court is not a panacea, it has proven remarkably successful in preserving and promoting Charleston's charm, and in 2004, the court was heralded by The United States Conference of Mayors and proclaimed a model for other cities.

CARDLOPOLIS
CONDITA A.D.
1670

LIVABILITY COURT

CITY OF CHARLESTON

OLD EXCHANGE

The vanguard of colony autonomy, a dank purgatory for criminals who
awaited their fateful walk to the gallows,
and host of a winsome four-day extravaganza during the dawning of the United
States that welcomed President George
Washington to town, the amount of history that has tread across the purbeck
floor of the Old Exchange and Provost
Dungeon earns its
status as one of the
city's most hallowed
buildings and one
of the preeminent
structures of Colonial
America.

**Old Exchange and
Provost Dungeon
122 East Bay
Street
www.oldexchange
.com
(843) 727-2165**

Election of delegates to the First Con-
tinental Congress; drafting of the first
constitution—the formal rebuke of
British control; and the ratification of
the U.S. Constitution all took place in
the Great Hall.

With two years as Commander in
Chief behind him, President George
Washington sailed into town on May
2, 1791, and the pag-
eantry that ensued
was unlike anything
Charleston—a city
notorious for its frivol-
ity—had seen before.
Twelve men wearing
blue silk jackets and

Its location as
the bookend of Broad Street, with one
side addressing the industrious wharves
and the other facing the city's main
thoroughfares, meant the Old Exchange
was perfectly situated to govern the
ever-growing shipping trade. Elegant
Georgian symmetry, Venetian windows,
and an octagonal cupola made it the
darling of the social set, but it was the
expansive room on the second floor,
ideal for august assemblies, that lion-
ized the building for the era's politicos.

black Florentine breeches rowed Washington to the landing, and a joyous
uproar coursed across the wharf when
he stepped ashore. St. Michael's church
bells rang wildly and a fifteen-gun *feu
de joie* crackled through the air. Legions
of elected officials paraded through the
city, delivering Washington and his
claque to the Old Exchange, where the
president was feted in true Charleston
style with two dinners, a concert, and a
ball over the course of four days.

SWEETGRASS BASKETS

Woven by the weathered hands of fieldworkers, the winnowing basket, a shallow sieve used to separate the chaff from the rice seed, is one of the oldest handcrafts of African origin in the United States. Fashioned from indigenous bulrush, a strong yet supple grass that thrives in the sandy soil associated with the leeward side of the coastal dunes system, the aroma of which—a near-cloying bouquet of fresh hay, thick with sweet, earthen notes—is indelibly associated with life in the Lowcountry. Golden strands of the dried grass, imbued with generations of wisdom and skill, give rise to sundry shapes and styles that draw a parallel to snowflakes: No two are exactly the same.

Every basket begins with a knot. Coils of the bundled grass are sewn together with thin strips of palmetto leaves or long-leaf pine needles to form a base. The basket then becomes an

Sweetgrass
Cultural Arts
Festival
www.sweetgrass
festival.org

evolution of the weaver's artistry. Early baskets were created to satisfy storage needs, but today's iterations are both utilitarian and stylistically complex, intended to hold fruit, bread, casseroles, magazines, and even jewelry. The sewing of sweetgrass is not just a functional skill, it's a venerable centuries-old art form that has been recorded into the annals of the Smithsonian Museum and was recognized as one of America's ancestral treasures in 2008 when the John D. and Catherine T. MacArthur Foundation commended sixty-three-year-old basket-weaver Mary Jackson with a $500,000 fellowship.

Baskets can be found at the City Market, but the best place to view the range of contemporary basketry is at the Sweetgrass Cultural Arts Festival, which is held prior to the grass harvest every June.

FESTIVALS

Gaiety galore! The panache with which Charleston throws a multiday celebration is spectacular. Throughout the year, the streets are atwitter with an elysian mode of life, and the city is alive with performances and parties.

The kickoff of Charleston's annual slate of revelry is both good-humored and record-setting; some of the nation's sharpest wits heat up local venues during the Charleston Comedy Fest, while more than 65,000 pounds of steamed bivalves entice thousands to brave the often-blustery January weather and eat their fill at the world's largest oyster roast. The plaintive wail of a slide guitar and the shrill cry of a bobcat blanket the city during February's Lowcountry Blues Bash and the Southeastern Wildlife Expo.

Come March, gastronomes parse the city's wide spectrum of cuisine, fashionistas flock to the runway, green thumbs are nourished, purveyors acquire antediluvian objects, and thousands admire local relics during the Charleston Food + Wine Festival, Charleston Fashion Week, Charleston Garden Festival, Charleston International Antiques Show, and the Festival of Houses and Gardens.

For timely festival information, visit www.charleston citypaper.com and www.charleston cvb.com.

Everyone heads outdoors in April to enjoy the Cooper River Bridge Run, Azalea Festival, Family Circle Cup, Charleston Greek Festival, East Coast Canoe and Kayak Festival, Charleston Race Week, and the Blessing of the Fleet. But on the off chance of rain, there's always the indoor refuge of the Charleston International Film Festival.

May ushers in the coronation of the city's premier arts fetes—the internationally renowned Spoleto Festival USA and the spirited Piccolo Spoleto. Estival winds mark the arrival of the harvest during June's Sweetgrass Cultural Arts Festival while also delivering a majestic fleet of tall ships to the Charleston Harbor Fest. September is soundly lyrical as the call of bagpipes and fiddles lures folks to the Scottish Games and Highland Gatherings, and the harmonious convergence of Caribbean music, gospel, and jazz defines MOJA, a celebration of African-American culture. The merriment concludes with the Holiday Festival of Lights, a wonderland of illumination that transforms a county park for three months beginning in early November.

CISTERN YARD

So named for its creation as a rainwater reservoir, the Cistern Yard is a verdant sanctuary set amid the bustle of an active student body. Although the mischievous tradition of dunking freshmen faded from popularity in the early 1900s, its air of higher learning and its historic setting make the stately greensward—cloaked in mature oaks and dissevered by moss-hewn stone walks—the heart of the oldest municipal college in the United States.

Constructed sixty-seven years after the College of Charleston's founding in 1857, the Cistern has historically served as the center of social life. In the 1920s "cisterning," or spending time at the Cistern in order to meet boys, was the height of fraternization for coeds. Today, the time-honored tradition of holding commencement exercises on Mother's Day, female graduates robed in white dresses and males clad in summer tuxedos, paints

College of
Charleston
66 George Street
www.cofc.edu

a picturesque diorama of education in the south.

Presiding over the grounds is an imposing russet-colored Greek Revival administration building, its pediment piazza and six Ionic columns grace the school's stationery. Entrance to the Cistern is gained through Porter's Lodge, the similarly florid-hued stucco gatehouse that for many years housed the college's sole janitor, who supplemented his annual salary of $800 by keeping a cow, chickens, and goats on the Cistern lawn.

The buzz of bright lights and cameras has dazzled students and inquisitive locals on numerous occasions as the Cistern played the role of idyllic backdrop in major motion pictures, including *Cold Mountain*, *The Patriot*, and *The Notebook*. This typically quiet lawn was also the site of a momentum-igniting event when Senator John Kerry formally endorsed Senator Barack Obama's bid for the presidency during a live broadcast in January 2008.

CHARLESTON RECEIPTS

Dozens of party punch recipes—Cotillion Club Punch, St. Cecilia Punch, Charleston Light Dragoon Punch, and the like—dot the first five pages of this storied cookbook, which hints to the verve with which Charlestonians like to entertain. Described by in the December 2002 issue of *Food and Wine* as "reflecting the nostalgia for the Old-South that prevailed among low-country aristocrats during the postwar (Civil War) era," *Charleston Receipts* is the authoritative volume of the city's heirloom recipes. The gustatory triumph with 750 recipes packed into 350 pages leads cooks on a savory tour of Charleston's culinary evolution from cooter stew to shrimp canapés. First published in 1950 by a group of enterprising members of the Junior League of Charleston who wished to raise funds in support of the Charleston Speech and Hearing Center, the book is now on

The Junior
League of
Charleston, Inc.
www.jlcharleston
.org
(843) 763-5284

Receipt vs. Recipe

Throughout this book, as you will see,
We never mention *recipe,*—
The reason being that we felt,
(Though well aware how it is spelt!),
That it is modern and not meet
To use in place of old *receipt*
To designate time-honored dishes
According to ancestral wishes.

L. F. K.

COOK BOOK COMMITTEE
The Sustaining Members of the Junior League of Charle

EDITORS

Anne Mont
...een Huguenin

its thirty-second printing. With more than 750,000 copies in circulation, a dog-eared copy of the unmistakable green, spiral-bound cookbook is an ubiquitous fixture in kitchens across the south.

Questionably named dishes, including Jellied Chicken Loaf and Baked Calf's Head, and comestible ingredients that seem foreign to pedestrian palates, like possum and turtle, share pages with victuals prized by Charlestonians: cheese straws, chow chow, shrimp pate, pickled okra, and Huguenot Torte.

Interspersed with entertaining bons mots—*Never call it "Hominy Grits," Or you will give Charlestonians fits!*—and colorful Gullah verses, the book exudes quaint charm. As for the chapter of party punch receipts, the Gullah wisdom warns, *"Ef yuh teck a heapa haa'd likker, yuh gwine tink deep en' talk strong."*

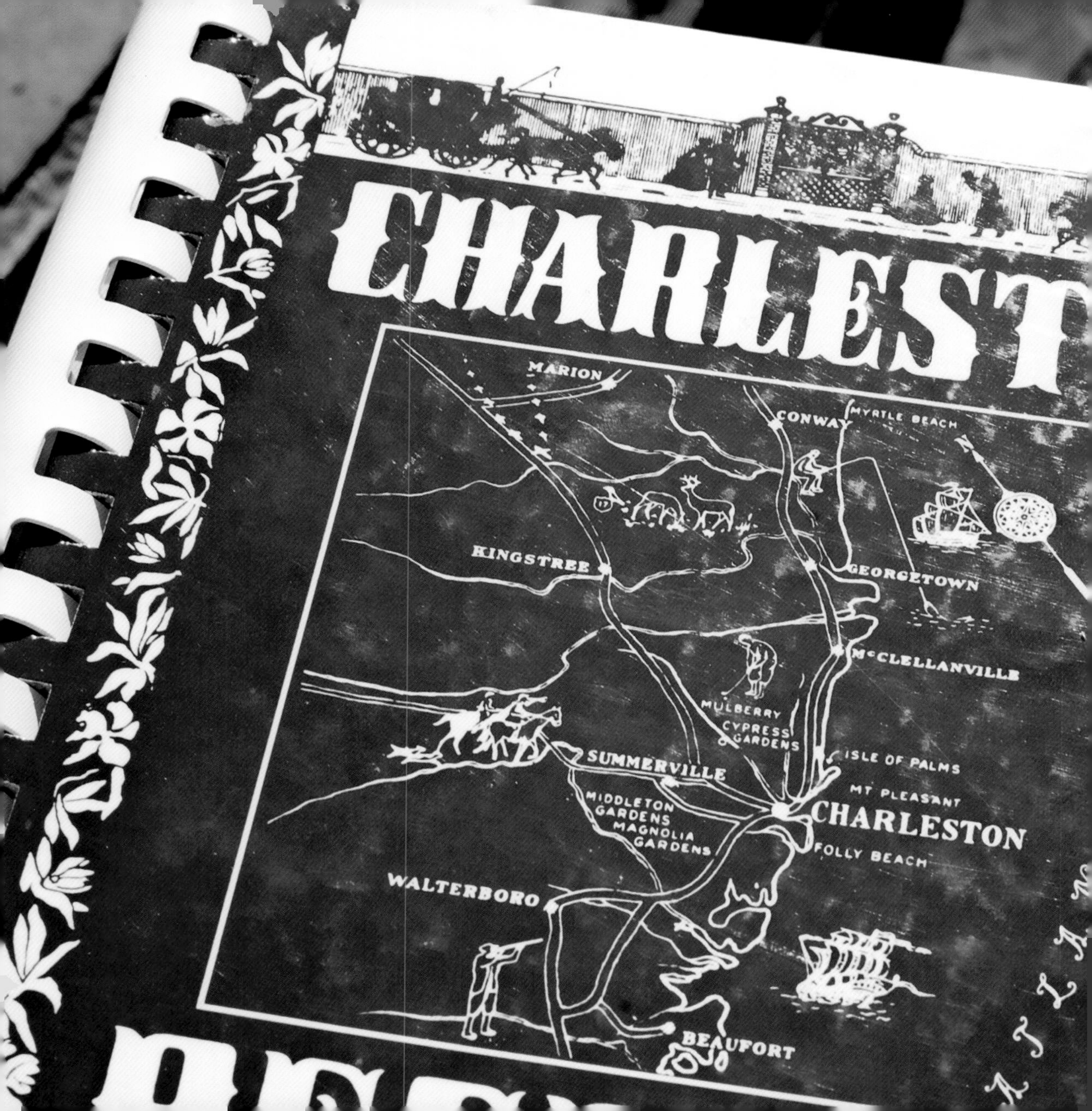

CHARLEST

MARION

CONWAY MYRTLE BEACH

KINGSTREE

GEORGETOWN

McCLELLANVILLE

MULBERRY
CYPRESS
GARDENS

SUMMERVILLE

ISLE OF PALMS

MT PLEASANT

MIDDLETON
GARDENS
MAGNOLIA
GARDENS

CHARLESTON

FOLLY BEACH

WALTERBORO

BEAUFORT

BENNE SEED WAFERS

Whisper-thin, buttery-smooth, and said to bring about good luck, benne seed wafers have appeared in Charleston larders since the heirloom recipe arrived via West Africa in the seventeenth century. Benne, the Bantu word for sesame, played a pivotal role in the cuisine of the Niger-Congo region, but the nutty-flavored seed was a novel, exotic ingredient for the English palate. Roasting intensifies the richness of the small seeds, making them an ideal flavor enhancer for an otherwise bland diet, and they quickly found their way into Lowcountry cuisine, most notably as the key ingredient in the sweet and savory benne seed wafer confection. It was an instant hit, so much so that it earned the honor of being the first food recipe

Olde Colony Bakery
www.oldecolonybakery.com
(800) 722-9932

listed in the wildly successful *Charleston Receipts* cookbook, the definitive collection of local "receipts."

The crunchy wafers are the preferred cocktail party petit four and sometimes served with pimento cheese in a coupling of two true southern delights. The sand-colored wafers also find themselves the unexpected ingredient in dishes such as oyster stew and breaded sea bass.

The Olde Colony Bakery has been selling the wafers since 1919, and packages of the distinctive Charleston treat can also be purchased at the City Market. A straightforward recipe incorporating little more than butter, sugar, flour, eggs, vanilla, and sesame seeds, a batch of the delectable delights can be whipped up in less than thirty minutes.

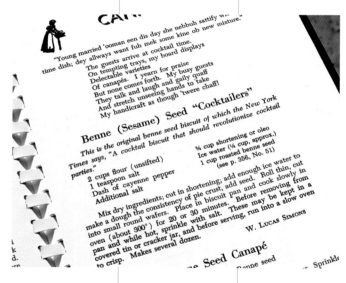

"Young married 'ooman een dis day she nebbuh sattify wid time dish; dey allways want fuh mek some kine ob new mixture."

The guests arrive at cocktail time.
On tempting trays, my board displays
Delectable varieties
Of canapés. I yearn for praise
But none comes forth. My busy guests
They talk and laugh and gaily quaff
And stretch unseeing hands to take
My handicraft as though 'twere chaff!

Benne (Sesame) Seed "Cocktailers"

This is the original benne seed biscuit of which the New York *Times* says, "A cocktail biscuit that should revolutionize cocktail parties."

2 cups flour (unsifted)
1 teaspoon salt
Dash of cayenne pepper
Additional salt

¾ cup shortening or oleo
Ice water (¼ cup, approx.)
1 cup roasted benne seed
(see p. 356, No. 51)

Mix dry ingredients; cut in shortening; add enough ice water to make a dough the consistency of pie crust, add seed. Roll thin, cut into small round wafers. Place in biscuit pan and cook slowly in oven (about 300°) for 20 or 30 minutes. Before removing from pan and while hot, sprinkle with salt. These may be kept in a covered tin or cracker jar, and before serving, run into a slow oven to crisp. Makes several dozen.

W. LUCAS SIMONS

ACE BASIN AND
FRANCIS MARION NATIONAL FOREST

Serpentine tributaries entwine virgin woodlands in both the ACE Basin and Francis Marion National Forest, large parcels of protected land that stand against the rampant development that has claimed many other parts of the Atlantic seaboard.

An aerial view reveals the diaphanous contours of the watershed responsible for the rise of Charleston, where tidal flooding nurtured plantation crops and floated raw goods to the port. The basin is a lush fantasia with a palette of celadon, russet, and cerulean hues that have long tantalized the plein air artists whose galleries populate Charleston's French Quarter.

Consisting of tidal marshes, wetlands, hardwood and upland forest, and shrubland, and named for the three rivers that lend their loamy banks to the boundary of the basin—Ashepoo, Com-

ACE Basin
www.acebasin
.fws.gov

Francis Marion
National Forest
www.www.fs.fed
.us/r8/fms

bahee, and Edisto—the ACE Basin National Wildlife Refuge represents a bulwark partnership by conservation groups, government agencies, and citizens to protect more than 350,000 acres, the largest undeveloped tract of wetlands on the East Coast.

At 250,000 acres, the Francis Marion National Forest trails the ACE Basin in size but more than makes up for it with a robust slate of recreational activities and vibrant wildlife that includes beavers, black bears, bobcats, and coyotes. Named for Revolutionary War general Francis "Swamp Fox" Marion, the strategy genius who sought refuge in the protective den of the cypress swamp between his guerilla warfare attacks and was immortalized by Mel Gibson in the film *The Patriot,* the forest is also home to the colorfully named Hellhole Swamp.